HAIKU

•

The Poetry of Zen

Edited by Manuela Dunn Mascetti
Introduction by T. H. Barrett

NEW YORK

For information address:
Hyperion, 114 Fifth Avenue, New York, NY 10011

ISBN 0-7868-6251-3

Designed by Gautier Design, London
Image selection by Timeless Enterprise (UK) Ltd., London

Library of Congress Cataloging-in-Publication Data
Haiku: the poetry of Zen / edited by Manuela Dunn; introduction by T.H. Barrett. — [1st ed.]
    p.   cm. — (A Box of Zen)
    ISBN 0-7868-6251-3
    1. Haiku—Translations into English. 2. Zen poetry, Japanese—Translations into English.
3. Seasons—Poetry. I. Dunn, Manuela, 1965– . II. Barrett, Timothy Hugh.
III. Series: Box of Zen.
PL782.E3H24 1996
895.6'1008—dc20   96–33723
                                                                                        CIP

Printed and bound in the United States of America by Quebecor-Kingsport
FIRST EDITION
10 9 8 7 6 5 4 3 2 1

CONTENTS

INTRODUCTION

In the West "less is more" is a maxim that has only been articulated in our century, but the traditional Japanese practice of writing haiku shows that this principle has long been understood elsewhere. At seventeen syllables there is no room at all for error in its limited compass, but in the good haiku that is space enough for much more than may meet the eye at first reading. Perhaps this has something to do with the history of the poetic form, which only achieved its complete independence as recently as the nineteenth century, since by origin the haiku derives from an element in the Japanese "linked verse" composed by two or more authors, the meaning of whose lines might be radically modified by the next contribution in the sequence. But surely there is more to this than the mere fact that the haiku was first shaped to fit more than one context: surely in this "less is more" poetics there is no little hint of Zen?

There can be no doubt of this in the case of Basho, who famously described his itinerant, ascetic existence as "neither monk nor layman." But what, for example, of Buson, who seems to model himself much more on the image of the Chinese gentleman-poet? We should remember that over the thousand years or so that Chinese poetry had influenced Japan by his time, it was the Buddhist poets who were the most appreciated, and in the days when linked

verse rose to prominence it was Zen monks who were responsible for diffusing a knowledge of continental poetry throughout Japan. The Chinese writers with whom the Zen monks were most familiar, for that matter, whether Buddhist or not, frequently drew analogies between poetry and Zen.

If, moreover, we trace such analogies back, it would seem that Buddhists of earlier times—when much Chinese poetry was inspired by heavy alcohol consumption—were concerned to propose as an alternative model of inspiration the heightened sense of reality achieved in meditation, no doubt very much to the advantage of East Asian poetry as a whole, and the haiku in particular. For though this form inherited an entire range of poetic conventions from earlier linked verse—from the use of season words to the format of the paper used to write the poem on—it still makes sense to speak of realism in the haiku, especially when the clear-eyed observation of ordinary life so typical of Basho plainly goes beyond anything in the more courtly environment of earlier poetry. And if, as the old Zen saying has it, "drawing water and carrying firewood" are the very activities in which supernatural power may be found, then we may well believe that it was not until the emergence of the haiku that this truth found its most telling realization in poetic form.

T. H. Barrett
Professor of East Asian History
School of Oriental and African Studies
University of London

THE ART
OF HAIKU

A monk once asked his Master, "No matter what lies ahead, what is the Way?" The Master quickly replied, "The Way is your daily life." This concept is at the very center of the Way of Zen. The principles that govern the Way are directed toward all of our existence, not just to the part that takes place in the meditation hall. The challenge of Zen is to meet each day, each moment with a clear mind and a cleansed spirit, so that the moment to moment union with existence becomes the highest teaching. This is the heartbeat that makes Zen today just as significant as when it was first brought from India to China by the wandering monk Bodhidharma in the year 520.

Zen has many flowerings, arts, and disciplines to which the Way (*do*) has been applied to create yet other forms of meditation and learning: *chado*, the way of tea; *kado*, the way of flowers; *kendo*, the way of the sword; *kyudo*, Zen archery; *judo*, Zen self-defense; *shodo*, Zen calligraphy. The underlying dynamism of all these arts is the full perception of the moment—being *here* and *now*—and this force is nowhere made more profound than in the subtle art of haiku.

Haiku is a poetic form which developed in Japan toward the closing of the seventeenth century. It consists of three phrases—or lines—of five, seven, and five syllables. Its popularity in Japan as a classic, and the enduring form in

which it is held in the highest esteem, lies in its nature and in the aesthetic principles that govern it. A haiku is like a vortex of energy; a haiku moment is a moment of absolute intensity in which the poet's grasp of his intuition is complete and the image he describes lives its own life. The art of haiku is to frame reality in a single instant that will lock the poet and the reader into sharing the same experience. It is this thunderbolt-like encounter that has made haiku the poetry of Zen—it is the voicing of those moments that cannot be described in prose or logic. This poetic form has breathing beauty and a moving elusive quality—reading it increases our sense of tranquillity and joy.

Haiku may be a more recent development of an extremely ancient form of Japanese poetry, called *katauta*, used to convey the utterances of the gods. The basis for *katauta* used to be the question-and-answer play of one god with another, which was reenacted by men and women at fertility and seasonal festivals. *Katauta* follows the same haiku pattern of 5-7-5 syllables, for a total of seventeen syllables, which is exactly the length of one human breath. The play between gods and spirits, thus, occurred in one breath, in one instant; and it is this same time frame that haiku has perfected to the ultimate art—the haiku moment. When we happen to see a beautiful sunset or lovely flowers we are often so delighted that we merely stand still. This state of mind might be

called "ah-ness" as we, the beholder, can only give a one-breath-long exclamation of delight: "Ah!" The object has seized us, we are being held, and we are aware only of the shapes, the colors, the shadows, and the blendings. In a brief moment we see a pattern, a significance we had not seen before. To render such a moment is the intent of all haiku, and the discipline of the form. Haiku poetry is a rendering of an experience, not a comment upon it. The closest approach toward a description of this art is to liken the process to the

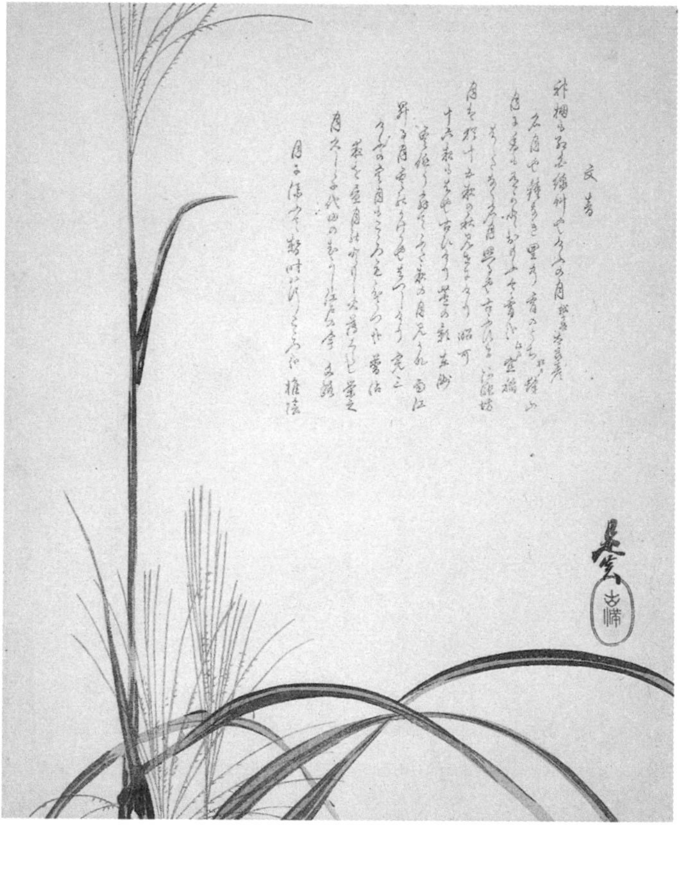

aesthetic appreciation of a painting in which contemplation and experience are one and the same consciousness. Every word in a haiku, rather than *contributing* to the meaning, like words do in a novel or sonnet, *is* an experience. Freshness is the flower of haiku art, for it is created by the immediacy of feeling. This gives the reader a true and everlasting delight; haiku can be read again and again without growing stale.

The haiku experience is made from three elements—where, what, when—which are bound in and with emotion to create a crystallized whole. In well-executed haiku, the elements of place, object, and time are so unified and so immovable that they create in the reader a nirvana-like sense. The key to understanding the skill of the poet is in the realization that in this art the artist strives always for the absolute. Of the absolute there is no question of degree; it is either attained or lost, just like a Zen experience. Most often it is not attained, and it is this constant striving toward and awareness of that high goal that has given strength to the aesthetic spirit that inhabits haiku.

Today in Japan, haiku is more popular than ever. The shortest form of poetry in the world is being adapted to our time and the wave of spiritual renewal it is bringing. Contemporary haiku reveals the skill of modern poets to remind us of the traditional, and now slightly anachronistic, "old Japan" of tatami mats, bamboo flutes, and shrines dedicated to the gods, and, almost as polar opposite, of the new awareness and possibilities emerging in our fast-changing culture. Themes of light and shadow, sound and silence in modern haiku reveal a fascination with spatial sense and acceptance of universal forces in keeping with the formal traditions of

an age now past. Other modern haiku poets, instead, break away from tradition by structuring their verses on anything other than the 5-7-5 syllabic form and by choosing themes unrelated to the natural world and the beauty of the changing seasons. As always, mastering the art of haiku takes years of practice. Japanese society considers that haiku poets do not attain maturity in this art until age 65, and many poets are well over 50 years old. Still, Japan has thousands of amateur haiku poets, and many experts in other professions write poetry as a hobby. A few thousand professional poets write, teach, appear on

TV and radio, and publish magazines. Haiku today has crossed the borders of Japan into the West and a few English poets and Zen adepts, especially in the United States, are attempting to compose verse by basing their work on the traditional Japanese form and content.

This volume presents selections from Matsuo Basho (1644–94), who was the first poet to develop the art of haiku, and his famed successors, Yosa Buson (1718–83) and Kobayashi Issa (1763–1827). These three are considered the first masters of haiku poetry. It also includes haiku by contemporary poets Natsume Soseki (1867–1916) and Toshimi Horiuchi, as well as classic verses by Hakuin, Ikkyu, Ryokan, and many other greats of the past. This volume further contains selections from contemporary Japanese women's poetry—Iida Dakotsu (b. 1914), Kimiko Itami (b. 1925), Sonoko Nakamura (b. 1913), Koko Kato (b. 1931), and Keiko Ito (b. 1935)—whose work is beginning to be translated into English for the first time. Not all the haiku selected for this volume follow the strict 5-7-5 syllable rule; these parameters were either lost in the translation from the original Japanese, or the poets decided to break away from this format and attempted innovation on the classical form. Haiku are inseparable from the changing seasons, and the poems in this book fall into the four traditional categories of spring, summer, autumn, and winter.

SPRING

Covered with flowers
Instantly I'd like to die
In this dream of ours!

ETSUJIN

Sitting silently,
Doing nothing,
Spring comes,
And the grass grows by itself.

OSHO

In the rains of spring
An umbrella and raincoat
Pass by, conversing.

YOSA BUSON

The mother crow
Walks forward with her child
Following behind.

NARUSE OTOSHI

On the spring equinox
Clouds perambulate
Around the entrance of
a mountain temple.

IIDA DAKOTSU

Spring rain:
Come inside my nightgown,
You nightingale, too.

NATSUME SOSEKI

Like the sound of a fire crackling:
River snow,
Melting.

KEIKO ITO

With one another
Let's play; O sparrow
Who has no mother.

KOBAYASHI ISSA

How clear and sweet
The water of the mountain to
An evening pilgrim.

KAMIO KUMIKO

Amid the green broad expanse
Mount Fuji clouded over
By the spring storm.

MORI SUMIO

Plum flower temple:
Voices rise
From the foothills.

NATSUME SOSEKI

A single petal
Of the cherry blossom fell:
Mountain silence.

KENNETH TANEMURA

My mother's soul
Viewing the plum blossoms,
Returning at night.

NOBUKO KATSURA

Buddha Law,
Shining
In a leaf dew.

KOBAYASHI ISSA

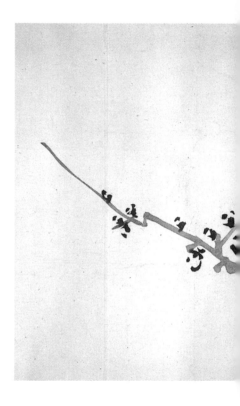

What a long spring day!
Catching yawns from one another
We go each our way.

NATSUME SOSEKI

Brushing the leaves, fell
A white camellia blossom
Into the dark well.

BASHO

SUMMER

Under a blazing sky
A sail in the distance—
The sail in my heart.

YAMAGUCHI SEISHI

As I turn over
In the fresh smell of straw mat
Summer has begun.

YE QIAN-YA

Watch birth and death:
The lotus has already
Opened its flower.

NATSUME SOSEKI

"Summer thinness, dear,"
I replied to him and then
Could not check a tear.

KIGIN

Flickering campfire—
I kneel by the mountain spring
For a drink of stars.

CHARLES B. DICKSON

The lamp once out
Cool stars enter
The window frame.

NATSUME SOSEKI

Don't weep, insects—
Lovers, stars themselves,
Must part.

KOBAYASHI ISSA

A fractured rainbow
Is staining under thunder clouds with
Cathedral quiet.

JAMES KIRKUP

A red sun
Falls into the sea:
What summer heat!

NATSUME SOSEKI

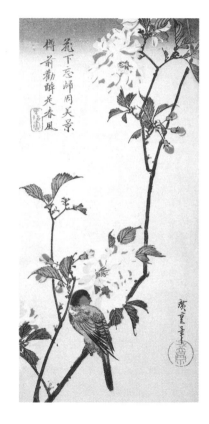

*Skylark
Sings all day,
And day not long enough.*

BASHO

*In the cicada's cry
There is no sign that can foretell
How soon it must die.*

BASHO

*My dead mother
Frequents my mind:
Wardrobe-changing season.*

NATSUME SOSEKI

"Look, O look, there go
Fireflies," I would like to say—
But I am alone.

TAIGI

Where there are humans
You'll find flies,
And Buddhas.

KOBAYASHI ISSA

Are there
Short-cuts in the sky,
Summer moon?

LADY SUTE-JO

Weaving thoughts
Of cotton—
Summer solstice woman.

KIMIKO ITAMI

Autumn

On a withered bough
A crow alone is perching;
Autumn evening now.

BASHO

The wild geese take flight
Low along the railroad tracks
In the moonlit night.

SHIKI

Morning glory:
A beauty's charm
But a few days' dream.

NATSUME SOSEKI

Full autumn moon—
On the straw mat,
Pine shadow.

KIKAKU

Autumn afternoon...
Without a ripple three white clouds
Cross the pond.

PATRICIA NEUBAUMER

Even the dumplings
Are smaller—
Autumn wind.

KYOROKU

Such a moon—
Even the thief
pauses to sing.

    BUSON

O leaves, ask the breeze
Which of you will scatter first
From the verdant trees.

NATSUME SOSEKI

Fallen leaves—
Raking,
Yet not raking.

    TAIGI

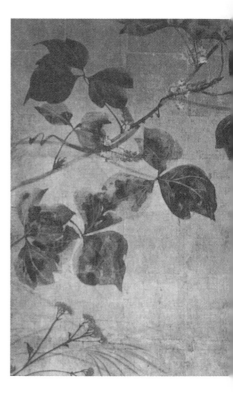

40

Autumn evening—
Knees in arms,
Like a saint.

KOBAYASHI ISSA

In the twilight gloom
Of the redwood and the pine
Some wisterias bloom.

SHIHOTA

Night frost—
Pulsing wings
Of mandarin ducks.

SOGI

A bell always rings
At dusk
In the water.

SONOKO NAKAMURA

Smell of autumn—
Heart longs
For the four-mat room.

BASHO

Storm—chestnuts
Race along
The bamboo porch.

SHIKI

The eyes of a stag
Listening to and feeling
Rising autumn wind.

FUKUDA KINEO

Wind in the West,
Fallen leaves
Gathering in the East.

BUSON

WINTER

Come, let's go
Snow-viewing
Till we're buried.

BASHO

Such silence:
Snow tracing wings
Of mandarin ducks.

SHIKI

Just by being,
I'm here—
In snow-fall.

KOBAYASHI ISSA

Not knowing why,
I feel attached to this world
Where we come only to die.

NATSUME SOSEKI

Wintry day,
On my horse
A frozen shadow.

BASHO

Through snow,
Lights of homes
That slammed their gates on me.

BUSON

Willow-trees are bare—
Dried the water, and the stones
Lie scattered here and there.

BUSON

Cold, yes,
But don't test
The fire, snow Buddha.

SOKAN

Living in the town
One must have money even
To melt the snow down!

KOBAYASHI ISSA

Confined within doors
A priest is warming himself
Burning a Buddha statue.

NATSUME SOSEKI

Winter well:
A bucketful
Of starlight.

HORIUCHI TOSHIMI

At the winter solstice
The sun permeates the firmament
Of the mountain province.

IIDA DAKOTSU

See the river flow
In a long unbroken line
On the field of snow.

BONCHO

What is your
Original Nature,
Snowman?

NATSUME SOSEKI

Glittering flakes:
The wind is breaking
Frozen moonlight.

HORIUCHI TOSHIMI

Miles of frost—
On the lake
The moon's my own.

BUSON

Outside the window, snow;
A woman in a hot bath
Overflowing.

NOBUKO KATSURA

Year's end—
Still in straw hat
And sandals.

BASHO

LIST OF COLOUR PLATES

Front cover-detail from Chrysanthemums by a stream with rocks by Ito Jakuchu, (c) *Museum of the Imperial Collections, His Majesty the Emperor of Japan, Kyoto*

ACKNOWLEDGMENTS

The editors gratefully acknowledge the following sources:

Zen Haiku, Soiku Shigematsu, trans. and ed., Weatherhill, New York

The Japanese Haiku, Kenneth Yasuda, Charles E. Tuttle Co., Inc. of Tokyo

The Penguin Book of Zen Poetry, Lucien Stryk and Takashi Ikemoto, eds. and trans., Penguin Books, London

A Long Rainy Season, Leza Lowitz, Miuki Aoyama and Akemi Tomioka, eds. and trans., Stone Bridge Press, Berkeley

Lowitz, Leza, Miuki Aoyama, and Akemi Tomioka, eds. and trans. *A Long Rainy Season-Contemporary Japanese Women's Poetry*, Vol. I. Berkeley: Stone Bridge Press, 1994.

Soseki, *Zen Haiku. Soiku Shigematsu*, trans. New York: Weatherhill, 1994.

Stryk, Lucien and Takashi Ikemoto, eds. and trans. *The Penguin Book of Zen Poetry*. London: Penguin Books, 1981.

Yasuda, Kenneth. *The Japanese Haiku*. Rutland and Tokyo: Charles E. Tuttle Co., 1957.

Kato, Koko, ed. *Four Seasons—Haiku Anthology Classified by Season.*
Tokyo: Ko Poetry Association, 1991.

Lowitz, Leza, Miyuki Aoyama, and Akemi Tomioka, eds. and trans.
A Long Rainy Season—Contemporary Japanese Women's Poetry.
Vol. I. Berkeley: Stone Bridge Press, 1994.

Miura, Yuzuru, trans. *Classic Haiku—A Master's Selection.*
Rutland and Tokyo: Charles E. Tuttle Co., 1991.

Osho. Hyakujo: *The Everest of Zen, With Basho's Haikus.*
Poona, India: Osho Foundation International.

Rengetsu. *Lotus Moon.* John Stevens, trans. New York: Weatherhill, 1994.

Stevens, John. *Three Zen Masters—Ikkyu, Hakuin, Ryokan.*
Tokyo, New York, London: Kodansha International, 1993.

Soseki. *Zen Haiku.* Soiku Shigematsu, trans. New York: Weatherhill, 1994.

Stryk, Lucien and Takashi Ikemoto, eds.and trans.
The Penguin Book of Zen Poetry. London: Penguin Books, 1981.

Yasuda, Kenneth. *The Japanese Haiku.*
Rutland and Tokyo: Charles E. Tuttle Co., 1957.

Ueda, Makoto. *Basho and His Interpreters.*
Stanford: Stanford University Press, 1992.

Manuela Dunn Mascetti is the author of *The Song of Eve, Saints, Goddess,* and coauthor with Peter Lorie of *The Quotable Spirit*. A Zen student of many years, she lives in London with her husband and her two Tiffanies named after Zen monks.

Professor Timothy Hugh Barrett, formerly Head of the History Department at the prestigious London School of Oriental and African Studies, is an expert on East Asian History who has studied Zen in both Japan and China for many years.